HAVE YOU BEEN FISHING LATELY?
Winning Souls for Christ

ANGELA R. CAMON

Edited By
Carl Camon, Sr.

Order this book online at www.trafford.com
or email orders@trafford.com

Most Trafford titles are also available at major online book retailers.

Printed in the United States of America.

ISBN: 978-1-4269-3434-6 (sc)
ISBN: 978-1-4269-3435-3 (e)

*Our mission is to efficiently provide the world's finest, most comprehensive
book publishing service, enabling every author to experience success.
To find out how to publish your book, your way, and have it available
worldwide, visit us online at www.trafford.com*

Trafford rev. 04/20/2011

 www.trafford.com

North America & international
toll-free: 1 888 232 4444 (USA & Canada)
phone: 250 383 6864 ♦ fax: 812 355 4082

Dedication

THIS BOOK IS DEDICATED TO every born again believer who evangelizes the lost, fulfills the Great Commission and reaches the world for Christ, and to those who have a desire to become a soul winner. It is also dedicated to those who have received encouragement by reading this book and as a result have made the decision to live a life for Christ.

Acknowledgements

I GIVE PRAISE AND HONOR TO my Lord and Savior Jesus Christ, the perfect soul winner. I am honored that God chose me to write this book about soul winning. To my husband Carl, thank you for your support and encouragement. Thanks for standing by me. I love you. To my four children, Carl Jr., Aaron, Camille and Candace. I count it a privilege to be your mother. To my parents, Rev. Dr. Vickery F. Williams and the late Pauline F. Williams, thanks for teaching me the word of God and leading me to Jesus. To my sisters, Tracie Davis, Vickie Smith and Kyna Williams, you are my sisters and my friend. I am blessed to have each of you in my life.

To my pastor, Pastor Madine Camon, thanks for setting an awesome example of being an effective soul winner. I love you. To my dear friend Jamie Christopher, I am blessed to have you in my life. I am honored to call you my friend.

Contents

Introduction

Generally when we think of fishing, we think in terms of fishing for bass, trout, snapper or some other type of fish. The activity of catching fish has been around for thousands of years and has become a favorite past time for so many. People fish for a number of reasons, some for the sheer pleasure of catching a fish, some for the enjoyment of participating in fishing tournaments, while others seek gainful employment as commercial fishermen. Whether we are fishermen ourselves or we know someone who enjoys fishing, I am sure we have all heard a fishing story or two along the way. The person telling the story does so, with much passion and excitement because he is eager to share about his success. This success brings him to a state of euphoria because his mission has been accomplished and that mission is to catch the most fish and the biggest fish. Once he has experienced the excitement and thrill of catching a fish, he will want to experience it again and again and again.

As children of God, we too should have a mission. Our mission is to fish for souls. We too should be filled with passion and excitement as we share our story and embark on our mission. While fishing in the natural sense may be viewed as a source of entertainment and may be taken lightly, fishing in the spiritual realm is of the utmost importance. Fishing for souls was and still is important to Jesus. He demonstrated this importance through his call to four fishermen, Peter, Andrew, James and John. Matthew 4:18-22 narrate the account of Jesus' call to these four fishermen into discipleship. According to verse 18, Jesus was walking by the Sea of Galilee, he saw Simon Peter and his brother Andrew, as they were casting their nets into the sea and said to them, "**Follow me and I will make you fishers of men**". They left their nets and followed him. Jesus called James, the son of Zebedee and John his brother, as they were in the ship mending their nets. They didn't hesitate and nor did they ask any questions, but they immediately followed Jesus.

Peter, Andrew, James and John were accustomed to fishing in the natural sense because they were seasoned fishermen by trade. They were used to casting their nets into the deep water generally at night and catching a school of fish, but in Luke the 5th chapter, Peter had a different fishing experience. He experienced the hand of God move in the miracle performed in catching a multitude of fish. Peter had been fishing all night and had not caught a single fish. Jesus told Peter to launch out into the deep and let down his net for a draught. Although Peter had been fishing all night and had not caught a fish, he was still obedient to Jesus. Peter let down the net and caught so many fish that he had to call for back up. He called fishermen from another boat to come and help him with the fish. They filled both boats with fish to the point that they had started to sink. Peter was so astonished at what he saw, that he told Jesus, "**Depart from me, for I am a**

sinful man, O Lord". Jesus told him, "**Fear not, from henceforth thou shalt catch men**". Fishing would never be the same for Peter, Andrew, James and John because Jesus was calling them into a spiritual endeavor. Their mission was to bring men into the kingdom of God. They were called to be spiritual fishermen.

God is calling all of us to be spiritual fishermen as well, and he is charging us with the same mission. We are commissioned to be kingdom builders and to win souls for Christ. It's time we go out into highways and hedges, and compel men, and women, boys and girls to come Jesus. Let's put the devil on the run and let him know that we have gone fishing.

Chapter 1

SOUL WINNING

JUST AS GOD WAS CALLING Peter, Andrew, James and John into discipleship, He is calling us too. He is calling us to be soul winners. Being a soul winner simply means to lead lost sinners to Jesus Christ for salvation. Many people feel that soul winning is only for missionaries, evangelists, pastors, or other church leaders. Perhaps they have arrived at this conclusion based on the scripture found in Ephesians 4:11-12, which states *"And he have some, apostles; and some prophets; and some evangelists; and some, pastors and teachers. For the perfecting of the saints, for the work of the ministry, for the edifying of the body of Christ"*.

This passage of scripture identifies some of the spiritual gifts given to Christians who functioned as apostles, prophets, evangelists, pastors and teachers for the perfecting of the saints. The Greek word for perfect means "to equip". So the purpose of these gifted individuals was to equip or train the saints for the work of the ministry to edify the church. While we each have been given a gift, soul winning is the responsibility of all Christians regardless of their spiritual gifts, offices or ministries. God has commissioned each of us to be soul winners, whether we are laymen or church leaders, new converts or seasoned saints.

Every Christian should consider soul winning as one of the highest honors, simply because it glorifies God. God is glorified when we tell others about His Son. It is a privilege to be an ambassador for Christ. Every part that we play in drawing people into the kingdom is an investment that will bring great rewards, even here on earth. **Daniel 12:3 "And they that be wise shall shine as the brightness of the firmament; and they that turn many to righteousness as the stars for ever and ever".** God will reward us both now and when we get to Heaven, if we win souls for Christ. There is no greater cause that we can devote ourselves to than winning souls for Christ.

In society, a person is considered to be wise if he or she can make a good business deal, or is financially savvy, or has the capability of grasping difficult or abstract concepts, but the bible declares that a person that wins souls is wise. **Proverbs 11:30 "The fruit of the righteous is a tree of life; and he that winneth souls is wise".** It does not matter what our occupation in society is, how educated we are, how rich, famous, or powerful we think that we are, how many political positions we hold, how many accolades we have received, or degrees we have obtained; there is no reward that compares the call of God to bring souls to Him.

Soul winning is a process of planting and harvesting. This process begins with the preparation of the soil. We must prepare the soil to receive the seed. As in the case of planting grass, flowers, vegetables and/or seeds, the preparation of the soil is the first step to reaping a great harvest. In the spiritual realm, we must prepare the soil (sinner's heart) through prayer. Intercessory prayer, which is praying to God on behalf of others, is essential in turning the hearts of sinners to Christ. We plant the seed (Word of God) in the heart of sinners. In the process of planting and harvesting, God may use more than one soul winner to witness to a person. The important thing to note is that it is God that draws them.

Paul said in **1 Corinthians 3: 6-8 I have planted, Apollos watered, but God gave the increase. So then neither is he that planteth anything, neither is he that watered: but God that giveth the increase. Now he that planteth and he that watereth are one, and every man shall receive his own reward according to his own labor.** God used Paul to plant the seed (Word of God), and Apollos to water the seed, but He gave the increase.

Whether God uses us to plant or if he uses us to harvest, we will all receive a reward for our labor. Our soul winning efforts are never in vain. You may witness to a sinner and they might not accept Jesus as their Lord and Savior at that moment, but another believer might witness to the same sinner, and lead the sinner to Christ. Another believer may indeed lead the sinner to Christ, but your efforts were not in vain because you sowed the seed in the heart of the sinner. It is never a waste of our time to witness to a sinner, because we never know which seed that was planted will lead to a born again believer.

Soul Winning Church

The mission of every ministry in every church should be soul winning. Unfortunately many churches have lost focus on the mission of winning souls for Christ. Some churches are not soul winning churches because the leaders and members have lost their passion for the lost. There is no burning desire in their hearts to see sinners come to Christ. It is because soul winning is not on the forefront of the churches agenda, but rather has been put on the back burner that sinners are not reached. Every church should strive to be a soul winning church. A church is successful in the eyes of God if its leaders and members are equipped to be soul winners.

The process of becoming a soul winning church starts with leadership. In order to be a soul winning church, the pastor must have the passion to be a fisher of men, in and out of the pulpit. If soul winning is not a joy or passion in the lives of leadership, then it most likely will not be in the lives of the followers. Not in all cases, but in many instances, members have a "follow the leader" type mentality, meaning that they do what the pastor does and what he or she teaches. If the pastor stresses the importance of being actively engaged in winning souls, then the members are more likely to be engaged in winning souls for Christ.

Sadly, too many pastors are stressing the importance of fishing for members instead of fishing for souls. Please don't misunderstand me, I am a pastor and I am in full support of encouraging people to join the church because I believe that every person needs a church home. But as leaders, we should not push membership over salvation. We need to let the sinner know that it is not enough just to be a member of a church, but he or she needs to be saved. It is more important that a sinner have his name written in the Lamb's Book of Life, rather than written on the church roll.

Soul Winning in Action

Throughout the book of Acts are several eye witnessing accounts of soul winning in action. Acts 2 gives a depiction of a remarkable and phenomenal event known as the Day of Pentecost. The Day of Pentecost played an important role in the early church following the resurrection of Jesus Christ. On the Day of Pentecost, the apostles came together in one place on one accord. A mighty rushing wind came and filled the house, and cloven tongues like fire sat upon each of them. The Holy Ghost came upon them and they began to miraculously utter forth the wonderful works of God in other languages. The people were amazed at how every man was speaking in his own tongue. Some alluded to the assumption that they were drunk with wine. Peter addressed the crowd and explained that it was the third hour of the day and that the men were not drunk. He spoke about the prophecy of the prophet Joel. "**And it shall come to in the last days, saith God, I will pour out of my spirit upon all flesh and your sons and your daughters shall prophesy, and your young men shall see visions and your old men shall dream dreams. And on my servants and on my handmaidens I will pour out in those days of my spirit; and they shall prophesy. And I will show wonders in heaven above, and signs in the earth beneath; blood and fire and vapor of smoke: The sun shall be turned into darkness, and the moon into blood, before that**

great and notable day of the Lord come. And it shall come to pass that whosoever shall call on the name of the Lord shall be saved". Peter concluded his sermon with the appeal to repent and be baptized and receive the gift of the Holy Ghost. After Peter's sermons, 3000 souls were saved.

Another example of soul winning in action is recorded in Acts 8:5-13. Philip was of the seven chosen by the Jerusalem church to assist the apostles in the administration of daily affairs. Not only did Philip assist in taking care of the physical needs, but he was also a spirit filled evangelist who led souls to Christ. In Acts the 8th chapter, verses 5-13, Philip preached the gospel in Samaria, and as a result God performed miracles causing many people to be healed and delivered from evil spirits.

There was a man by the name of Simon who practiced sorcery. He boasted about how great he was, and had many followers, from the least to the greatest. The people who followed him thought that he was the great power of God because they were amazed at his magical performances. But when Philip preached the things concerning the kingdom of God and the name of Jesus Christ, the people believed and were baptized. Simon also believed and was baptized. He followed Philip everywhere and was amazed by the great signs and miracles that he saw.

In verses 26-40 in the 8th chapter of Acts, God orchestrated a divine appointment to use Philip to lead an eunuch to Christ. An angel of the Lord spoke to Philip and said, **"Arise and go toward the south unto the way that goeth down from Jerusalem unto Gaza, which is desert".** Philip started on his journey and on his way he met an Ethiopian eunuch who was an important official in charge of all the treasury of Candace, queen of the Ethiopians. This eunuch had gone to Jerusalem to worship and on his way home he was sitting in his chariot reading the book of Isaiah the prophet. The Spirit told Philip to go to the chariot and stay near it. Philip heard the man reading and asked him, "**Understandest thou what thou readest**?" In other words, Philip was asking the man do you understand what you are reading? The eunuch responded by saying, "**how can I except someone guide me**". He then invited Philip into his chariot and he read the passage of scripture. Philip started with that same scripture and preached the good news about Jesus.

As they traveled along the road, they came to some water and the eunuch asked to be baptized. After Philip baptized the eunuch, the spirit of the Lord took him away. The eunuch went on his way rejoicing.

Acts the 9th chapter illustrates the transformation of Saul to Paul. Saul was an enemy of the church and a persecutor of its believers. **Acts 8:3 says "As for Saul, he made havoc of the church, entering into every house, and haling men and women committed them to prison."**

Saul went to the chief priests and got permission to go to Damascus to search for Christians with the intent of finding them and bringing them back to Jerusalem to prison. As he was traveling to Damascus, a bright light surrounded him. Saul fell to the earth and heard a voice say **"Saul, Saul why persecutest thou me?"** (Acts 9:4)

Saul asked, "**Who art thou Lord?**" Jesus then told him that he was **Jesus, whom thou persecutest. (Acts 9:5)** Jesus instructed Saul to continue to go to Damascus and he would be told what to do. After receiving instructions from Jesus, Saul arose from the ground and discovered that he was blind. He was blind and he didn't eat or drink for three days.

Now Ananias comes on the scene. Ananias, a believer who lived in Damascus, had an encounter with Jesus through a vision. The Lord spoke to him and told him to go to Straight Street, to the home of Judas, where he would find Saul of Tarsus. Ananias was afraid because of Saul's history of persecuting believers. But God reassured Ananias and told him, **"Go thy way: for he is a chosen vessel unto me, to bear my name before the Gentiles, and kings, and the children of Israel." (Acts 15)** With belief of what God had told him, Ananias proceeded to Damascus and found Saul. He laid hands on Saul, the scales fell from his eyes and his sight was restored. Saul was filled with the Holy Ghost and baptized. The disciples were skeptical of his conversion. They couldn't believe that he was a disciple because they remembered what he had done in the past. They were so afraid that they plotted to kill him. But Barnabas took him and told the disciples how Saul had seen the Lord and that the Lord had spoken to him and how he had boldly preached in the name of Jesus Christ.

Acts chapter 10 gives an account of the conversion of Cornelius and his household. Cornelius was a devout man who feared God. He was a generous giver and a man of prayer. The Bible says that Cornelius always prayed to God. One day Cornelius saw in a vision, an angel coming to him and calling his name. Cornelius asked, **What is it Lord**? The Lord told him that his prayers and alms had come up for a memorial. The angel of the Lord told Cornelius to call for Simon Peter and he would tell him what to do. He was then instructed to send men to Joppa and to call Simon Peter. Meanwhile, Peter went on the house top to pray. He became hungry, but he didn't eat because he fell in a trance. In his vision, Peter saw heaven open up and certain vessels descending to him. He saw four footed beast, wild beasts, creeping things and fowls of the air. While Peter was pondering over the vision, the Holy Spirit spoke to him and told him that three men were seeking him. These men, who were the men that Cornelius had sent, explained to Peter that Cornelius had been instructed by an angel to hear the words of God through him. Cornelius gathered his family and his friends, and they all listened as Peter preached. As Peter was preaching the Holy Ghost fell on all of them, which heard the word. They were all amazed because the Holy Ghost was upon the Gentiles. One aspect that makes this case unique in that Cornelius was the first Gentile to whom the gospel was preached.

A lesson that we can learn from Cornelius' life is that although he was a good person, gave alms, had reverence for God, and even prayed, he still needed salvation. His good works could not save him; he was saved only after he heard the gospel of Jesus Christ. The fact of the matter is that there are a lot of good people on their way to hell. Religion, doing good deeds or being a good person can never supersede salvation.

Requirements To Be A Soul Winner

Many people feel as though they are not qualified to be a soul winner because they are considered by some as a babe in Christ, or because they think that they don't have enough knowledge to lead a soul to Christ. If you have accepted Jesus Christ as your Lord and Savior, then you have met the requirement to be a soul winner. Even if you are a babe in Christ, you can still share your testimony. You have what it takes to reach souls. We are all equipped to be soul winners, but there are some things that we need to bear in mind if we want to be effective at this endeavor.

1. **We must stay committed to being a soul winner**. We must make ourselves available to God so we can take advantage of every soul winning opportunity. Soul winning should be a daily part of our routine.

2. **We must be willing to go to the lost**. In most cases the sinner is not going to come to the believer and ask to be saved. The believer must be willing to reach out to the sinner and meet him or her on his or her territory. This means that you may have to step out of your comfort zone to reach a sinner.

3. **We must maintain an active prayer life.** We must communicate with God. We have to stay connected to God through prayer. It is God who touches the hearts of men and women for salvation. He is the only one who knows who is ready to accept the Gospel Plan of Salvation. We should pray for opportunities to witness for Christ and have a listening spirit when he answers. The more time we spend with God in prayer and studying his word, the more fruit we will bear and the more souls we will win.

4. **We must understand the sinner**. In order to understand the sinner, you must be able to

identify with the sinner. You need to understand the sinner's spiritual condition to help them move from where they are to where they need to be. They need to be in a relationship with Jesus. Many of us seem not to be able to identify with sinners now that we are saved. We have been saved for so long, until we have forgotten what it was like to be lost. Apparently, some of us have become too "spiritually deep" to remember what the struggle was like for us, before we were called out of the darkness into the marvelous light. You will never be successful at being a soul winner, until you have an understanding of how a sinner thinks and acts. Paul understood the importance of identifying with the sinner.

Paul said in 1 Corinthians 9:19-22 "*For though I be free from all men, yet have I made myself servant unto all, that I might gain the more. And unto the Jews I became as a Jew; that I might gain the Jews; to them that are under the law, as under the law that I might gain them that are the law. To them that are without law, as without law (being not without law to God, but under the law to Christ) that I might gain them that are without law. To the weak became I as weak, that I might gain the weak: I am made all things to all men: that I might by all means save some*". Paul's interest was to preach the gospel and win men to Jesus Christ. He was willing to sacrifice his own personal freedom, so that he could win more souls.

The Perfect Soul Winner

Jesus Christ was the perfect soul winner in the Bible. He went everywhere preaching, spreading the Gospel in every village, and in every town. He preached on a mountainside, on the sea, in the desert, and in the wilderness. Jesus came to be a soul winner. **Luke 19:10 says "For the Son of man is come to seek and to save that which was lost".**

Jesus was the perfect soul winner because he had compassion for the lost. He emphasized the value of a lost soul by the illustration of his three parables of the lost sheep, the lost coin and the lost son in Luke the 15th chapter. It was paramount that Jesus used these parables to demonstrate God's top priority with one soul who is lost. Jesus is still passionate and concerned about the sinner today. He does not want any sinner to perish.

As we study the ministry of Jesus, we find that he ministered to the whole person. He oftentimes began with helping people deal with their hurts, needs and interest. He witnessed to them and met their needs at the same time. His main objective was to bring them to a right relationship with God, but he met their needs first. In John 8:1-38, Jesus healed a man blind from birth by spitting on the ground, making clay of the spit, and then anointing the man's eyes with the clay. He told the man to **"go wash in the pool of Siloam"**. After he washed in the pool, he could see. The man was healed. It was after the fact that Jesus took care of the man's physical need that he asked him if he believed on the Son of God.

Jesus was the perfect soul winner because he was not a condemner. Jesus didn't come to condemn sinners, but he came to save them. Paul said in **1 Timothy**

1:15, "**This is the faithful saying, and worthy of all acceptation, that Christ Jesus came into the world to save sinners, of whom I am chief**". He did not come to point fingers and find faults. Jesus exercised forgiveness to the adulteress woman in John the 8th chapter. Jesus went to the Mount of Olives, and it was there that the scribes and Pharisees brought a woman who was caught in the very act of adultery. According the law it was commanded that such an act would require that the woman be stoned, but the Pharisees and scribes inquired of Jesus of what should be done to the woman. They were seeking to trick Jesus to see whether he would uphold the law or defend the sinner. Jesus stooped down and with his finger wrote on the ground as though he didn't hear them. They continued to ask Jesus what they should do. Jesus stood up and said, "**He that is without sin among you**, **let him first cast a stone at her**". (**John 8:7**) He then stooped down again and wrote on the ground. They were all convicted by their conscience and each left one by one, leaving only the woman and Jesus. Jesus lifted up and saw that everyone had left. He asked her "**Woman where are those thine accusers? hath no man condemned thee? (John 8:10).** The woman told him that no one had condemned her. Jesus told her "**neither do I condemn thee: go and sin no more**" **(John 8:11).**

Because of the fact that Jesus does not condemn us for our sins, does not indicate that he condones sin. But he understands that the sin, such as in the case of the woman caught in adultery, was not the problem, but it was a symptom of the problem. Sin, whether it is drug addiction, adultery, pornography, lying, stealing or any other sin, is not the problem, but a symptom of the problem. The root of the problem is that the sinner is not in the right relationship with God. Jesus deals with the root of the problem.

Finally, Jesus can be described as the perfect soul winner because he was known to be a friend of the sinners. Take a look at John 4:4-42 when the Samaritan woman had an encounter with Jesus. The events that led to her conversion started with Jesus going through Samaria and making contact with a Samaritan woman at the well. He did the most unusual thing and asked her for a drink. It was unusual for a Jewish person to ask for a favor or accept a drink from a Samaritan's cup. Jesus spoke to her need and revealed Himself as the Messiah. She believed. She witnessed to others and led them to Christ.

Another example is Jesus and Levi, the tax collector, as recorded in Luke 5:27-32. Jesus saw Levi at the tax office and he said **"Follow me".** Levi followed Jesus, made a great feast in his house for Jesus and invited others to come as well. The religious leaders criticized Jesus for having contact with sinners. Jesus said to his critics, **"They that are whole need not a physician, but they that are sick; I came not to call the righteous, but sinners to repentance".**

As Jesus walked through the streets of Jericho, he met a man named Zaccheus. Zaccheus can be identified as a chief tax collector who was rich and little in stature. Zaccheus wanted to see Jesus, but he was not able to because of his height. In his desperation to see Jesus, he climbed a sycamore tree. Jesus looked up and said **"Zaccheus, make haste, and come down; for today I must abide at thy house.** Zaccheus came down. Because Jesus went to Zaccheus's house, he was once again criticized by religious leaders. Jesus always embraced sinners and we should follow his example.

Chapter 2

WHY SHOULD YOU BE A SOUL WINNER

PERHAPS YOU MIGHT BE THINKING to yourself, why should I have to be a soul winner, aren't there already enough people on the battlefield to win souls for Christ? Well, according to what Jesus said in **Matthew 9:37 "The harvest truly is plenteous, but the laborers are few";** there are not enough people on the battlefield fighting for lost souls to come to Jesus. That is why you and I must be about our Father's business, and that business is to build the Kingdom of God.

To answer the question, why we should be soul winners is quite simple. One of the main reasons that we should be soul winners is because it glorifies God. Actually nothing glorifies God more than the conversion of a sinner. Jesus said in Luke 15:7 ***"I say unto you, that likewise joy shall be in heaven over one sinner that repenteth, more than over ninety and nine just persons, which need no repentance".*** The angels in heaven rejoice when even one sinner repents and turns to Christ. When we take our responsibility of bringing souls to Christ seriously, this brings glory to God.

Another reason that we should be soul winners is because we are commanded by God to fulfill the Great Commission. The Great Commission is one of the most significant passages in the Bible and is the basis for soul winning. It is significant because it is the last recorded personal directive that Jesus gave to his disciples. Before he ascended into heaven, Jesus commanded his disciples to **"go and make disciples of all nations, baptizing them in the name of the Father and of the Son and of the Holy Spirit, and teaching them to obey everything that I have commanded. And surely I am with you alway to the very end of the age (Matthew 28: 19-20)."** Jesus has commissioned each of us to the call of fulfilling the Great Commission. He is calling us to step out in faith and spread the gospel of Jesus Christ. Whether we share the good news with our next door neighbor, or travel to a remote region of the world, where ever we are called, as believers we are compelled through obedience to share the gospel. We must tell non-believers the message of Jesus' death, burial and resurrection for their sins. According to Luke 24:47 repentance and forgiveness of sins is to be preached. We are to preach the good news with the goal of leading sinners to believe, and as a result of preaching the gospel disciples are made.

Thirdly, we should be soul winners because hell is real. Hell was created as a place of judgment for Satan and those who follow him in their rebellion against God. **Revelation 20:10 says "And the devil that deceived them was cast into the lake of fire and brimstone,**

where the beast and the false prophet are, and shall be tormented day and night forever and ever. Every sinner that does not repent of his sin will spend eternity in the lake of fire. **Revelation 20:15, "And whosoever was not found written in the book of life, was cast in the lake of fire**." Hell was not created for us, but rather it was prepared for the devil and his angels (Matthew 25:41). God does not want anyone to perish and go to hell. According to **II Peter the 3:9, The Lord is not slack concerning his promise as some men count slackness, but is long-suffering to us-ward, not willing that any should perish, but that all should come to repentance.** He would rather for us to accept his son Jesus and go to the place that he has prepared for us called heaven. **John 14:2-3 says, In my Father's house are many mansions, if it were not so, I would have told you. I go to prepare a place for you. And if I go and prepare a place for you, I will come again and receive you unto myself; that where I am, there ye may be also.** Every day someone goes to hell. Think for a moment of the number of people who will be in hell because we didn't take the time to share the gospel of Jesus Christ.

I can recall an incident about a lady who struggled with the issue of finding the time to witness to her neighbor. She knew that she should witness to him, but she couldn't seem to find the time. Between fulfilling her roles as a wife, mother and school teacher and serving in many ministries in her church, she didn't have much time for anything else. As each day pass by she would promise herself that she would find the time to witness to her neighbor. One day as she was leaving to go to work, she saw her neighbor in his yard. She felt a strong sense of urgency to tell him about Jesus. But she dismissed this feeling and decided to go to work so she wouldn't be late. She did however promise herself that she would witness to him that evening when she returned home. Unfortunately that was one promise that she was not able to keep. As she was coming home from work she saw an ambulance headed toward her neighborhood. Not only was the ambulance coming to her neighborhood, but it was headed to her neighbor's house. According to medical records, her neighbor had a massive heart attack. He had died without her ever telling him about Jesus.

There is a story recorded in the book of Luke 16:19-31 that highlights two main characters, the rich man and Lazarus. The rich man was clothed in purple and favored sumptuously every day. While Lazarus, a beggar full of sores, laid at the gate desiring to be fed the crumbs from the rich man's table. Both men died, and Lazarus was carried away in Abraham's bosom, but the rich man went to hell. The Bible says, **"in hell he lift up his eyes, being in torments"**. In much pain and agony, the rich man requested of Abraham to let Lazarus dip the tip of his finger in the water so that he could cool his tongue. In response to the rich man's request, Abraham brought to his remembrance of the lifestyle that he once lived and the lifestyle Lazarus had lived. The rich man had received good things in life, while Lazarus had received evil things. But now the roles were reversed because the rich man was tormented and Lazarus was comforted. The rich man didn't want his five brothers to come where he was, so he wanted to send Lazarus on a mission to testify to them. Abraham said that they had Moses to warn them, and if they were going to heed to a warning they would have to hear it from Moses. Assuming that his brothers would not heed to Moses' warning, he suggested that if a person came from the dead to warn them, they would be more receptive of the message. I want to encourage you to do everything in your power to warn as many people as you can before they die. We must witness to others about Jesus Christ, and if they accept him as their personal savior, they can spend eternity with him, but if they do not, hell will be their final destination.

Fourthly, we should be soul winners because Satan is real. Satan was an angel who rebelled against God and was cast out of heaven. **Isaiah 14:12 says, "How art thou fallen from heaven, O Lucifer, son of the morning! how art thou cut down to the ground, which didst weaken the nations.** Satan let pride get in his way and wanted to take God's position. He failed but his mission is still the same. He still wants to take God's place. Of course we know that he can't take God's place, but he tries to stop the will of God. He does everything in his power to stop men and women from accepting Jesus Christ as their Savior. According to **II Corinthians 4:4, Satan seeks to blind the minds of men so that they will not believe the gospel.** Satan is real and he is on his job. His mission is to destroy man. The bible warns us about Satan in **I Peter 5:8, which says, Be sober, be vigilant; because your adversary the devil, as a roaring lion, walketh about, seeking whom he may devour.** Satan is real and he is powerful, but he is powerless against God. We must warn lost sinners about his schemes and devices.

Chapter 3

WHY DON'T WE
WIN SOULS?

IF WE KNOW THAT WE should be soul winners, then why don't we witness? I am sure that there are many reasons why some people don't witness, but I think the number one reason is fear. Fear plays an intricate role in why Christians don't witness to sinners. What exactly do they fear? For some, the fear of being rejected, the fear of offending someone, and the fear of being a failure are some of the reasons why many people do not to witness.

Rejection is something that we don't enjoy. None of us like to face rejection of any kind for any reason. But when it comes to witnessing, we have to prepare for the possibility of the sinner rejecting our message. It would be wonderful if everyone that we witnessed too would make the decision to accept Jesus as Lord and Savior, but unfortunately there will be some who will reject the message that we are conveying. It is important that we stay in the right attitude and right frame of mind and not to allow ourselves feel offended because the sinner did not receive what we were saying. We shouldn't take rejection personally because the sinner is not really rejecting us, but rather he or she is rejecting God. God can handle rejection. He is not offended at all by the sinner's rejection because when he is ready to draw the sinner, he has the power to do it.

Another fear that causes Christians not to witness is the fear of offending someone. I have often heard Christians confess that they don't want to say anything to sinners because they are afraid that they will offend them. They don't want to make them mad and get involved in a confrontation. I believe that it is better to possibly offend someone and keep them from going to hell than to not say anything and let that person die and lose their soul.

The fact of the matter is that some people will be offended when you share the gospel because their sinful nature is being exposed. Some people are so deep rooted in their various religions and are very adamant about what they believe, that when the real truth is presented to them, they take offense. But regardless of the circumstances, we have to tell them the truth and lead them on the right path. For example; you and your friend are planning to go on a trip. Your friend decides that since he is a world class traveler, he should be the driver. With no hesitation, you agree to let him drive. After traveling a few miles, you detect that you all are going the wrong way. You inform your friend that you all are headed in the wrong direction, but he is convinced that he knows the right way. Because you are looking at the map, you know that he is on the wrong road. You have two choices, you can either to let him travel in the wrong direction and continue to be lost or you can correct him in a loving way and encourage him to turn around and head in the right direction. As in the case of you and your friend, if we don't say anything the sinner will continue to be lost and travel in the wrong direction.

I am not advocating that it is okay to be offensive. That's not what I am saying at all because the Bible clearly warns us about being offensive to others. However, I am saying that soul winning is serious business and we can't take it too lightly.

Fear of failure plagues the minds of many Christians because we all want to successful at whatever task that we undertake. As humans, if we feel as though we are going to fail at a certain thing, even if it involves working for God, then often times we will not attempt it simply because we don't want to experience failure. As children of God we cannot afford to let the fear of failure be a determining factor of whether we will fulfill our responsibility as soul winners or not. Fear of failure is not an option for a child of God. The Bible states that God did not give us the spirit of fear but of power, love and sound mind. The word of God also states in Philippians 4:13, **I can do all things through Christ which strengthens me.** You and I have what it takes to be a soul winner. One way to help alleviate the fear of failure is to focus on the fact that it is the responsibility of the Holy Spirit to draw the sinner, not ours. Yes, we are responsible for witnessing, but ultimately it is the responsibility of the Holy Spirit to convert the sinner's heart.

Although fear is one of the most common reasons why Christians don't witness, there are others reasons as well. Among them are, Christians have become too complacent in their comfort zones. They have turned a deaf ear and a blind eye to the plight of the sinner and have become too apathetic about warning others about their sins. As a result, sinners remain lost and destined for hell. Some Christians will have few rewards when they get to heaven because they have allowed opportunity after opportunity to share the gospel of Jesus Christ pass them by.

It is sad that some Christians have grown cold in their love for Christ, which is another reason why we don't witness for Christ. In Revelation chapter 2, Jesus spoke to the church of Ephesus and told them that they had left their first love. That is exactly the way it is with some of us. We have left our first love. We have forgotten the joy we felt when we accepted Jesus in our hearts. We don't remember the zeal that we had to learn all that we could about Jesus and how we wanted to share what Jesus was doing in our lives. We have become too familiar with the life that we have now, since we have Jesus in our hearts. We can't seem to find the time to share with others.

Speaking of time, have you ever felt that you couldn't seem to find enough time in your schedule to witness? My friend, if your schedule is too tight for you to tell somebody about Jesus, then something is wrong. One thing is for sure is that your priorities are in the wrong order. It seems easy for us to find the time to follow our own passions, but we need to adjust our lives so that our passions are in line with God's passion. Time is a one of God's most valuable gifts. He wants us to be good stewards of the time that he has given us. Each of us is given an equal amount of time in a day. No one gets more time in a day than anyone else does. So, the underlying issue is not quantity of time, but rather the stewardship of time. If you have found that your schedule is too hectic for you to take the time to witness to others, then you need to reprioritize your schedule. God is holding us accountable for witnessing, and we can't let a lack of time be an excuse for not telling someone about Jesus.

I am quite sure that perhaps there are other personal reasons why some Christians choose not to witness, but regardless of the reason, it is not acceptable in God's eyesight. God will hold us accountable for every soul that we don't witness to. Take a look at what he told Ezekiel. "***Son of man, I have made you a watchmen for the house of Israel: so hear the word I speak and give them warning from me. When I say to a wicked man, You will surely die and you do not warn him or speak out to dissuade him from his evil ways in order to save his life, that wicked man will die for his sin, and I will hold you accountable for his blood. But if you do warn the wicked man and he does not turn from his wickedness or from his evil ways, he will die for his sin: but you will have saved yourself". (Ezekiel 33:7-9)*** As the Lord's watchmen, it is our responsibility to warn people of the danger of sin and to point them to God's mercy.

It is every Christian's responsibility to be a soul winner. Every Christian is commanded to be a witness for Christ. If we are not involved in reaching others with the gospel, then we are being disobedient to God.

Chapter 4

FISHING FOR SOULS

Now that we have learned that soul winning is important and that we will face some consequences if we do not win souls for Christ, it's time that we get prepared to start fishing. Fishing naturally and fishing spiritually share the same agenda in the respect that both are trying to catch something. In preparation for fishing in the natural aspect, there are several things that must be taken into account such as location, the type of bait that you will use, and the method that you will use to catch fish.

There are also various types of equipment that is needed, such as a pole, fishing line, a sinker, a bobber, a hook, and some bait. Although all of the equipment is important, the bait is very important because it is the bait that attracts the fish. You can sit on a bank of river all day, with a pole and no bait, and chances are you won't catch a fish. Some fish can be lured in using artificial bait, but the presence of live bait is a temptation that hardly any fish can resist. Regardless of the bait, whether artificial or live, you have to use something that gets the fish attention. Once you get the bait on the hook and cast the pole into the water, eventually the fish will bite and you will feel a tug on your pole and then you can reel the in the fish.

So it is with spiritual fishing, the bait is very important as well. As spiritual fishermen, we too must use bait that will get the attention of sinners. We should always use live bait and that is the living Word of God. Once we get the Word of God and cast it into the street corners, cast it into the drug houses, cast it into the night clubs, cast it into the schools, cast it into our churches, then eventually the sinner will bite the bait. You will feel a tug in your spirit and soul, then you can reel in the sinner. Just as we have to pull the fish out of the water, we have to pull the sinner out of hell, with the Word of God.

When we fish for souls, it helps first to define our target. We have to know who we are trying to catch. In this case, we are trying to catch (reach) lost souls. Although we are responsible for witnessing to all sinners, regardless of sex, gender, age, creed, color or nationality, a good practice is to identify a target of who you are trying to reach. For example, because of some of the things that I have experienced in my life, I have a passion to work with young teenagers; females in particular. Now that is not to say that I don't witness to others outside of that category because I do. This is just a good starting point for me.

Maybe you have a God given passion to work with people who have served or are serving time in prison. A good starting point for you would be to start a jail ministry by sharing the gospel of Jesus with the inmates in your local jail. Again we are responsible for witnessing to all sinners. It is our responsibility to fish for all lost souls. We are to fish for the drug addict who is strung out on crack. We are to fish for that single mom who has lost all hope. We are to fish for the homosexual who believes it is okay to be attracted to the same sex. We are to fish for that college student who seems to have a bright future ahead. We are to fish for that well dressed business man who is at the peak of his career. We are to fish for that person who thinks doing good deeds or just being nice is his ticket to heaven.

Secondly, when we go fishing for souls, we must go where the sinners are. Very rarely does a sinner come to you and ask about Jesus, so we must be prepared to go where he or she is. So where do we go to find sinners? Sinners are everywhere. They are in your home, your church, your community, your grocery store, your neighborhood park, in your school, at the night club, at the drug house, and the list goes on and on. We have to get out of our comfort zones and go where the sinners are.

Tools To Use For Fishing
Gospel Tracts

Distributing gospel tracts is a good starting point in your efforts to win souls for Christ. Tracts are very inexpensive and easy to use. They can be given directly to individuals or can be left in a public place, such as a shopping center or your favorite restaurant.

One-On-One Witnessing

One-on-one witnessing is used when one individual shares the gospel with another individual. This is an effective way to win souls because it allows the individual share openly, and feel comfortable in asking any questions that he or she may have.

Bible Studies

There is power in reading the Word of God. Studying the Word of God together is a fruitful way of winning souls. You can invite someone to your Bible Study at your church or you might even consider starting a bible study in your home.

Street Preaching

Street preaching can be an effective means of reaching lost souls for Christ. There are numerous examples throughout the Bible of how Jesus and so many others utilize street preaching as a means to reach sinners.

CD/DVD

Give out CDs/DVDs of your church service. The person can listen to the CD and watch the DVD, as many times as he or she would like and in the comfort of their own home.

Internet

The Internet can be used in many ways to proclaim the gospel of Jesus Christ. Using the Internet you can participate in forums to share your beliefs. If you have a favorite website you can create a link to those sites. You can use Facebook to share your testimony or your favorite scriptures or post a video on a video sharing website like You Tube. Another great way to share the gospel of Jesus Christ with everyone is using online video tracts. You can put them on your website or send them in an email.

Whatever we have access to, we can use as a means to witness for Christ. I had a unique opportunity to win a soul for Christ. A young lady had texted a message to my cell phone by mistake. She obviously thought that I was someone else because the message that she sent was very vulgar. Initially, I thought I would just ignore the message and go on, but then I thought what a great opportunity to share something about Jesus. I texted her back to inform her that she had mistakenly texted the wrong person. Then I asked who she was, and with no hesitation she told me. I said to her, "from reading your message it seems like you are having a rough day". From that point on, she shared with me why she was having a bad day. The conversation escalated to her telling me her life story. She shared with me about the guy that she was dating, which led me to believe that the relationship that she was involved in was unhealthy. After reading several of her texts messages, I finally texted her and told her about Jesus and how he wanted to have a relationship with her. I explained to her that with this relationship she would never have to worry about being disrespected. She would never have to second guess as to whether or not she was loved. She would be the apple of God's eye. We continued to text back and forth until eventually our conversation ended with her accepting Jesus as her personal Savior.

I think back on that day and often wonder what would have happened, if I had reacted in a different way. What if I had texted the young lady back and told her how offended I was because after all, I am a Christian. Shouldn't I be offended? I could have ridiculed her for using vulgar language, but instead the Holy Ghost led me to witness to her and as a result she replaced her old relationship with her boyfriend, with a new relationship with Jesus.

Chapter 5

BEING AN EFFECTIVE WITNESS

Aᴡɪᴛɴᴇss ɪs ᴀ ᴘᴇʀsᴏɴ ᴡʜᴏ can attest to a fact. The role of a witness in a court case is to testify to evidence that they have firsthand knowledge of. A witness's testimony is crucial to the outcome of a case. So it is with being a witness for Jesus Christ. Our testimony is crucial to the outcome of the sinner. So how can we be effective witnesses for Jesus? We can accomplish this by testifying to what we know Christ has done in our lives. In I John 1:1-3, John spoke about testifying to what you have seen and heard when he said **"That which was from the beginning, which we have heard, which we have seen with our eyes, which we have looked upon, and our hands have handled, of the Word of life. For the life was manifested, and we have seen it, and bear witness, and shew unto you that eternal life, which was with the Father, and was manifested unto us. That which we have seen and heard declare we unto you, that ye also may have fellowship with us: and truly our**

fellowship is with the Father, and with his Son Jesus Christ."

Being an effective witness does not require you to be an eloquent speaker nor does it require you to be a theologian, but you should be familiar enough with the Word of God so that you can effectively share it with others. In order to effectively share the Word of God, you must know the Word, and in order to know the Word, you must study the Word. According to **II Timothy 2:15, the Word encourages us to "study to shew thyself approved unto God, a workman that needeth not to be ashamed, rightly dividing the word of truth."** Committing soul winning scriptures to memory will help you prepare for witnessing opportunities.

An essential characteristic of an effective witness is being filled with the Holy Ghost. **Ephesians 5:18 says, "And be not drunk with wine, wherein is excess, but be filled with the Spirit."** We cannot be effective witnesses in our own strength; we must rely on the Holy Spirit's enabling power. In our own strength, we are helpless, spiritually impotent and fruitless. But when the Holy Spirit serves as our power source, we are empowered to be fruitful witnesses for Christ. According to Acts 1:8, we will receive power after we receive the Holy Ghost. **"But you shall receive power after that the Holy Ghost has come upon you: and ye shall be witnesses unto me both in Jerusalem, and in all Judea and in Samaria and unto the uttermost part of the earth."**

Prayer is vital to being an effective witness. It is important that the lines of communication between us and God stay open. We should actively engage in prayer for opportunities to witness. We also should pray for those individuals that the Holy Spirit has led us to witness to. An effective witness must have an active, fruitful prayer life. We should pray for opportunities to witness to others.

I am sure, many if not all of us have heard the phrase "your attitude determines your altitude." I believe that this applies to the case of being an effective witness. A positive attitude is a key component in being an effective witness. Having the right attitude when witnessing will draw sinners to God. The right attitude is one that operates out of love and compassion for the lost sinner. It is an attitude that is friendly and inviting. If the sinner feels comfortable around you, he is more likely to listen to your message. Although we should maintain a positive attitude when witnessing to the sinner, we still must speak the truth. We must speak the truth, so that the sinner can see his true spiritual condition, and not to try to prove a point or win an argument. Our job is not to judge, but it is to present the facts, and allow the Holy Spirit do his job to convict, convince and convert the sinner.

Finally, an effective witness can be identified as one who has surrendered his life to Christ and is sure of his own salvation. As Christians, we must completely surrender to the Spirit. We must commit our intellect, will and emotions to Jesus Christ. We can be sure of our own salvation by receiving the gift of God's love through Jesus Christ. We must confess any known sin and we should ask the Lord to search our hearts, so that he can reveal any hidden sin. We cannot be effective witnesses if we have not surrendered our lives or if we are not sure of our own salvation. We can only testify to what we have experienced. If you have not experienced God's love and forgiveness through his Son Jesus Christ, then you can't be a witness to that. We can't lead others to where we have not gone and are not willing to go.

Tips to Remember

Study and know God's Word
Be filled with the Holy Spirit
Keep an active prayer life
Seek and pray for opportunities
Depend on the Holy Spirit for guidance

Chapter 6

LET YOUR LIGHT SHINE

Iᴺ ꜱᴏ ᴍᴀɴʏ ᴄᴀꜱᴇꜱ, ᴛʜᴇ only bible that some people will ever read is the life that you live. People may never pick up the bible and read it, but they will make judgments and decisions about their lives based on how you live your life. That is why we need to make sure our lives are worth reading about. By the grace of God, we must reflect the Word and truth of God in the way we live our lives and conduct our affairs. People are always watching us to see if we are living a life that exemplifies a true child of God. Your attitude and Christian example must attract people to your lifestyle. They must see by your example that you are committed to the Lord. If you are filled with the Holy Spirit, then the fruit of the Spirit will be visible in your life.

I have encountered people who have given me a litany of excuses as to why they don't attend church, but one that I often hear the most is "nobody in the church is right." Of course that is an unfair statement to make because there are some true Christians who are living a holy and acceptable life unto God. However, there is some validity to what has been said. There are some people who live a hypocritical life. They say one thing and do another. Many people call themselves Christians, but they are not living the life of a Christian. They claim to know Jesus and have submitted a surrendered life to him, and yet they follow the pattern of the world. That is one example of being a hypocrite.

We must practice what we preach. As Christians, we cannot have the "do as I say, not as I do" mentality, but we must be committed to living a Godly life every day. The testimony of your life must be consistent with your words. The Word of God says, ***"Whosoever obeys the commandments and teaches others to do the same will be great in the kingdom of heaven."(Matthew 5:19)*** We first must obey, before we can teach others. One of the worst things that we can do is to preach what we don't practice. If we live our lives contrary to our testimony, we can't be effective witnesses.

If we live Godly lives, others will want to follow simply because they want what we have. I can remember a friend telling me about a lady on her job who was so mean to her. Every day she did all she could to try to make my friend upset. The more she tried to make her upset, the more my friend prayed for the lady. My friend continued to display her Christian disposition. This went on for a period of time, but eventually, the lady came to my friend and told her why she gave her a hard time. She said, "every time you come to work you always have a smile on your face. I don't understand how you could come to work so happy every day, while everyone else is so miserable with all the problems on the job." The lady confessed that she wanted my friend to be miserable, so she purposely treated her bad in any way that she could. The lady told my friend "it didn't matter how bad I treated you though, you always treated me nice." She said, "I don't understand, but I want to understand." That day my friend led that woman to Christ. Not only did my friend lead that lady to Christ, but she led so many others, just by letting her light shine. Think for a moment: what if my friend had decided not to let her light shine? What if she had retaliated against the lady on her job? That story would have definitely had a different outcome.

Now think for a moment would you have been able to win that lady to Christ if you were in my friend's position? How is your attitude in your work place? Is your attitude worth catching? Are you an infectious Christian? Is your faith contagious? These are some questions that we really need to ask ourselves on a regular basis. Many times it is the Christian who does the most complaining about changes on the job, pressures in life, and the downfall in the economy, instead of the sinner man or woman .

Did you know that sometimes we are judged by our reaction rather than by our action? Sinners watch how you react to situations. How do you respond when people are unkind to you? How do you react when someone cuts you off in traffic? How is your attitude when your boss tells you that you have to work longer hours with the same pay? What do you do when the server in a restaurant gets your order wrong? How is your attitude?

Have you ever taken the time to think about how many people you have kept from coming to Christ simply by your attitude? It is sad to think about it, but some of us have actually driven people away from Christ because of the way that we react in certain situations. As

Christians, our lives are studied and examined under a microscope for all the world to see. That is why we must be as shining lights in the world. **Philippians 2:15 says, "That ye may be blameless, and harmless, the sons of God, without rebuke, in the midst of a crooked and perverse nation, among whom ye shine as lights in the world."**

Chapter 7
SHARING YOUR TESTIMONY

Your testimony is evidence of what God has done in your life. It is a look back at where you have come from and where you are now. It is a story of how your life was before you accepted Christ, and what your life is like after you have accepted Christ. Every Christian has a testimony and every testimony is significant. Your testimony may consist of being delivered from a life of drug/alcohol addiction, prostitution, gambling addiction, while another Christian may have grown up in a Christian environment and never experienced that type of lifestyle. The fact of the matter is we were all sinners separated from God and on our way to hell. It is because of God's grace that we even have a testimony to share.

Your testimony has power. **Revelation 12:11 says, "And they overcame by the blood of the Lamb and the word of their testimony, and they loved not their lives unto the death".**

Sharing your testimony is a key element in winning souls for Christ. By sharing, many people who are facing situations that seem hopeless will discover that there is hope through Jesus Christ. Sinners need to hear your testimony so they will be inspired to seek God for themselves. Then they can experience the peace and satisfaction that comes along with having a relationship with Jesus. The more you share and talk about how God has intervened in your life, the more people will begin to realize that God is real, miracles do happen and prayer works. Not only will sharing your testimony offer encouragement to the sinner, it will give you an opportunity to reflect on what God has done in your life. Sharing with unbelievers is what we as believers have been called to do. God has given us the privilege of being His ambassadors so we should consider it an honor to share our testimony.

Everyone of us has a testimony, but not all of us are willing to share it for various reasons or another. Some perhaps don't share because they think their testimony is not significant enough. Again, everybody has a testimony and everybody's testimony is significant.

Some people are ashamed to tell of the things that God has delivered them from. I have a friend of mine who readily admitted that she did not feel comfortable sharing her testimony because she was embarrassed about some of the things that she had done in the past. She felt like she was being a hypocrite by telling others about sinning against God, when she in fact had sinned against Him for so many years. She didn't think it was her place to tell others about their sins. I explained to my friend that she was falling right into the enemy's trap. That was exactly the way he wanted her to think and feel. Because my friend has such an awesome testimony, Satan knew that if she shared her story, others would be delivered and set free. So he deceived her into thinking that she was being hypocritical in sharing about her life. I am pleased to say that my friend no longer carries the load of guilt and shame about her past, but instead praises God that her past is just that....the past. Her focus is not on the things that she used to do, but rather what she can do for Christ and that includes sharing her testimony.

Pointers For Sharing Your Testimony

Describe how your life was before you accepted Christ.
What motivated you to invite Christ into your life?
Describe how your life was after you accepted Christ.
How did your life change?

Chapter 8

SHOW LOVE

G OD HAS COMMISSIONED EACH OF us to love our
neighbors as ourselves. If we follow the principle of
showing love to others we can draw sinners. Too many
times we judge others and look down on them for the
mistakes that they have made instead of embracing them
with love. It is not to say that we must condone what
the person does, but you must accept the person for who
he is. The truth of the matter is we have all sinned and
fallen short of the glory of God and we all need his love
and grace. I often think about the exemplary love that
God showed for us. John 3:16 says, **"For God so loved
the world that he gave his only begotten son that
whosoever shall believe in him shall not perish, but
have everlasting life."**

God gave his only Son to die for us. The Bible
says in Romans 6:23 that **while we were yet sinners,
Christ died for us**. We were sinners and God showed
us love, therefore we should follow through with the
same concept and show love to others. God gave us the
ultimate example of drawing others by showing love.

I am convinced that a lot of souls are not being saved because too many Christians are not exemplifying the love that Christ has commanded. I think that sometimes we get too complacent with experiencing God's love for ourselves, that we forget about spreading His love abroad. Jesus died for everyone. Sometimes we want to pick and choose who we show love too.

I can recall an experience that one of my friends told me about. My friend had been living a lifestyle that consist of partying, drinking, smoking, having sex with several partners, staying out late and just not being responsible. Some of her relationships with her family members had been damaged due to some of her irresponsible actions. One day we were talking and she confided in me and told me that she was tired of living this lifestyle. She wanted to get her act together, as she stated, and start living a better life.

The first thing that she wanted to do was to start attending church. She decided that she was going to visit a church three blocks from where she lived. As she entered the church, she immediately felt the tension. People stared and barely spoke to her. The usher did not greet her in a friendly manner as she had done with the other visitors when she escorted them to their seats. The usher looked at my friend and told her, "you can just find a seat". She sat on the third pew in the middle section of the sanctuary, only to find out that she was sitting in Ms. C's usual seat. She was asked to move and told to sit on the back pew. One of the women in the church said, "honey you should know better than to come to church like that. I know you can dress better than that." My friend told me how bad that made her feel. She stayed for the remainder of the service, but she did not ever visit that church again.

Because my friend was really adamant about learning more about Jesus and living a better life, she found another church to attend. She decided to visit a church that had a small congregation, but a lot of love. This experience was different. As soon as she walked in she was greeted by the usher with a smile and was told that she was glad that she had come to visit their church. The usher escorted her to her seat. She immediately felt that she was welcome and felt a sense of acceptance. She was seated by a middle aged woman, who gave her a warm smile and a big hug, as if she already knew her.

My friend tried to apologize about the clothes that she had on, but the lady told her not to worry. She gave her a small piece of cloth to cover her legs because her dress was short. The lady said to her, I am more concerned about your heart than your clothes. She said, "when God touches your heart and saves you, all that will change (meaning the way she was dressed)." She said, "I am just glad you are here."

As the service went on, the choir sang songs about God's love and the preacher delivered a sermon about God's forgiveness. At the end of the sermon, the preacher extended the invitation for salvation. My friend told the lady seated next to her that she wanted to be saved, but was afraid to walk to the preacher in the front of the church. The lady walked with her, she accepted Jesus as her savior and she became a member of that church.

I asked her what was the deciding factor in why she joined that church, thinking that she would say the powerful sermon that the preacher had preached or maybe a song the choir had sung, but she said, "it was the smile" that got me. When the usher and that lady smiled at me it made me feel like they accepted me. Sometimes it is something as simple as a smile that will draw the attention of a sinner.

It's easy to love those who love us, but we are both called and commanded to love our enemies (Matthew 5:44). Jesus said in Luke 6:32-36, **"If you love those who love you, what thank (credit) have ye? For sinners also love those that love them. And if ye do good to them which do good to you, what thank have ye? for sinners also do even the same. And if ye lend to them of whom ye hope to receive, what thank have ye? for sinners also lend to sinners, to receive as much again. But love ye your enemies and do good, and lend, hoping for nothing again, and your reward shall be great, and ye shall be the children of the Highest; for he is kind unto the unthankful and to the evil."**

Acts of Kindness

Sometimes it is the smallest things that make the most difference in a person's life. I am a fanatic about sending cards because I am an encourager and I consider sending cards as part of my ministry. I like to encourage people. No, I love to encourage people. I like the joy of knowing that I have brighten someone's day or let them know that I was thinking about them and love them. I send cards for special occasions (birthdays, anniversaries, weddings, graduations, baby showers, etc.). My most favorite type of card to send is a "just because" card. This is the card that I send for no special reason, but just because.

One day I was praying and seeking God for direction about who I should send a card too. The Holy Spirit led me to send a card to lady who was a friend of mine. He told me to give a card that offered encouragement. I did not know the circumstances that this lady was facing. I did not know what she was going through, but God did. I didn't' question God as to why I needed to send the card. I just acted out of obedience. In response to the card, the lady wrote me a letter explaining everything that she was going through and how she was at the point of giving up. She was wavering in her faith and she just wanted to give up. The card that I sent encouraged her to continue her walk with the Lord.

Another time that I was led by the Holy Spirit was when I sent a card to a young lady who was contemplating suicide. Of course at the time I did not know that. Again I acted out of obedience, and on what the Holy Spirit instructed me to do. This young lady had fallen into the trap of Satan's schemes and felt that she had no other way of escape from the problems that she was facing. She said my card came when she was at her lowest point in her life. But after receiving the card, she knew that there was hope and that someone cared about her. She started going to church with me and she gave her life to the Lord. That one simple card helped to change her whole outlook on life.

Do you get my point in that sometimes it is the small things that make the most difference? Some people think that it takes a lot of money or you have to be in a prestigious position in order to make a difference, but all that it really takes is a willing mind and loving heart to make a difference in someone's life.

Showing love to sinners, is one of the highest callings of the Christian faith. So, let's get out of our comfort zones, and do as the bible has commanded us to do, and that is to love our neighbor as ourselves. Walking in love is the only way that we will see lives transformed.

Chapter 9

LEADING OTHERS
TO CHRIST

B EFORE WE TAP INTO OUR discussion on leading others
to Christ, I want to first establish the fact that it is
the Holy Spirit that draws a person to Christ, not us. We
are the instruments that God uses to bring that person to
Christ. When we bring a person to Christ, it is because
God is working through us. Secondly, only God knows
who is ready to accept Jesus as Savior. God knows whose
heart he has touched and made ready to hear and believe
the gospel. That is why it is important that we pray and
seek God for direction.

With an understanding that we are instruments
being used by God, and that it is the Holy Spirit that
converts a person, we will move further into discussion
of leading others to Christ. Our mission in evangelism,
or soul winning is to bring lost souls to the kingdom of
God. Building God's Kingdom should be the top priority
on every Christian's agenda. We should focus on building
His kingdom one soul at a time by presenting a living

Jesus to a dying world. So how do you lead a person to Christ? We start by presenting the gospel of Jesus Christ to the sinner. Whenever we present the gospel, there are four things that we should address, and they are salvation needed, salvation provided, salvation offered, and salvation received.

Salvation Needed

When presenting the gospel we must show the sinner that he needs to be saved. We must show him or her that without Jesus Christ they are lost sinners separated from God. The sinner must grasp the fact that they need Jesus or else they won't see the significance of being saved.

Salvation Provided

Because of Adam and Eve's rebellion against God, man was separated from God because of sin. God's holiness required punishment and payment for sin, which was eternal death. **Romans 6:23 says, For the wages of sin is death but the gift of God is eternal life**. Our death was not sufficient to cover the payment for sin. God required a perfect spotless sacrifice. Jesus gave his life as a ransom, as payment for our sins. Jesus Christ provided salvation for the sinner when He died for their sins.

Salvation Offered

God freely offers the gift of salvation through his son Jesus Christ. Salvation is God's gift to us, we cannot purchase this gift nor can we acquire it from our good deeds. *Ephesians 2:8-9 says, For by grace are ye saved through faith: and that not of yourselves; it is the gift of God. Not of works lest any man should boast.*

Salvation Received

God is offering the gift, but it is up to the sinner to receive it. God wants every sinner saved, but he gives each sinner the choice of whether he or she wants to accept His son Jesus.

The Road To Christ

When we travel, we need direction to help us get from one place to the next. Many of us have come to rely heavily on our GPS system to help us get to our destination. If our destination is to get to heaven, then we need some directions too. The book of Romans is referred to as the road map; it gives us the directions that we need to get to heaven. Several verses found in the book of Romans lead a clear path to Jesus. **Roman 3:10 - As it is written, there is none righteous, no, not one.**

Romans 3:23 -For all have sinned and come short of the glory of God.

Romans 6:23- For the wages of sin is death, but the gift of God is eternal life through Jesus Christ our Lord.

Romans 5:8 - But God commended his love toward us, in that while we were yet sinners, Christ died for us.

Romans 10:9&10-That if thou shalt confess with thy mouth the Lord Jesus and shalt believe in their heart

that God raised Jesus from the dead, thou shalt be saved. For with the heart man liveth unto righteousness, and with the mouth confession is made unto salvation. Romans 10:13- Whosoever shall call upon the name of the Lord shall be saved.

These verses provide the answers to why the sinner needs salvation, how it is being offered, and how they can receive it.

Our Message

Our message should always be about Jesus Christ. We must emphasize that Jesus Christ is the only way to salvation. Jesus said in **John 14:6, "I am the way, the truth and the life. No one comes to the Father except through me.".** The message that we should convey to sinners is that God loves them and wants them to be saved. According to **II Peter 3:9, "The Lord is not slack concerning his promise as some count slackness, but is long suffering to us-ward, not willing that any should perish, but that all should come to repentance."** Sinners need to hear the message that Jesus Christ died for our sins. He was buried. He was raised on the third day with all power in his hand.

There are many ways or approaches that we can use to lead someone to invite Jesus into their heart. One approach is the direct approach. The direct approach is when a Christian gets straight to the point. They may ask a question, "if you died tonight, do you know where you would spend eternity? On the other hand the indirect approach is when you start a conversation with the person, before mentioning anything about salvation. For example, you may start a conversation about the weather, or ask them a question about themselves. This is usually a good starting point, because most people like to talk about themselves. During the conversation, you can incorporate something about Jesus. A perfect example of this was when Jesus met the woman at the well. He started talking about water and used it as a starting point to bring the conversation to her spiritual need.

Examples of Leading Someone to Christ

You should use a method that you feel comfortable with, but more importantly you should rely on the Holy Spirit to lead and guide you as to how you should approach a sinner. Below is a example of how you can lead someone to Christ.

Step 1

You might want to start using a direct approach by asking a question such as Do you think there is a Heaven and Hell? or What are your spiritual beliefs? or perhaps you could start with the question, If you died right now, where would you spend eternity? The purpose of asking these questions is not to start a debate, but rather to give the person an opportunity to talk so that you can see where they are spiritually. If you are using the indirect approach, you might want to start the conversation by simply asking how they are doing, or any topic that they can relate to or might be interested in.

Step 2

The second step consists of reading the Bible. It is the word of God that changes people lives, therefore it is important that you give the person an opportunity to read scriptures that pertain to salvation, preferably out loud. A series of scriptures that can be used are Romans 3:23, Romans 6:23, John 3:3, John 14:6, Romans 10:9-10, II Corinthians 5:15, and Revelation 3:20.

Again it best for the person to read the Word for himself, but on the occasion that a person can't read or does not feel comfortable reading aloud, it is perfectly okay for you to read the scriptures to them.

Step 3

After reading the scriptures, ask the person is he willing to surrender his life to Christ? Or does he want to invite Jesus into his life and heart, as his Lord and Savior? If he answers yes to the questions, then proceed with prayer. Below is an example of a sinner's prayer.

Heavenly Father, I have sinned against you. I want forgiveness for my sins. I believe Jesus died on the cross for me and rose again. Father, I give my life to you, to do with as you please. I want Jesus Christ to come into my life and into my heart. This I pray in Jesus name, Amen.

Chapter 10
FOLLOW UP

WHEN I FOUND OUT THAT I was going to be a mother, I was both excited and scared because I realized both the joy and the responsibility that a baby would bring. Nevertheless, I made preparations for the new addition to our family. I read books so that I could learn as much as possible about taking care of a newborn baby. My husband and I got the baby's room ready for its arrival. I did everything I could possibly think of so I would be ready for that big day.

After nine months, which seemed like an eternity, it was finally time to deliver my baby. After much prayer and intense hours of pain, my baby was finally born. An overwhelming joy filled the room as my family and friends admired our new baby. Think about this for a moment. What if after going through the preparations to welcome my new baby in the world, and after going through hours and hours of intense labor pains, and after reading book after book to gain knowledge about being a mother, I suddenly decided to leave my baby at the hospital. Everyone would have thought that I had lost my mind, especially my husband. In many cases, that is what we do as believers. We make preparations to bring the new believer to Christ, and once they accept Christ, we lose connection with them. Some Christians have been misled into thinking that once a new believer has been led to Christ, then their mission has been accomplished, but that is only one aspect of the mission. Our work is just beginning.

We are now charged with the task of serving as a spiritual mom or dad or brother or sister to help the new convert grow in his faith. The process of helping a new believer grow can be identified as the follow up. It is essential that we follow up with every new believer because even before that person is led to Christ, Satan is on his job trying to bring doubt and confusion about the decision that the new believer has made. So what can you do to help the new believer?

Pray

It is important that we pray for the new believer on a regular basis. Jesus said in **Luke 22:31-32, "Simon, Simon behold Satan hath desired to have you, that he may sift you as wheat". But I have prayed for thee that thy faith fail not: and when thou art converted, strengthen thy brethren."**

Share the Word of God

In I Peter 2:2, a new convert is referred as a newborn babe. Just as a newborn babe needs nourishment to grow, a new convert needs spiritual nourishment to grow. The new convert, or newborn babe needs the sincere or pure milk of the Word of God, so that they can grow. The Word of God needs to be presented to the new believer so that he or she can digest it. As a parent, you would not give your newborn table food because his or her system cannot handle it. So it is with the spiritual babe, he or she must be given the Word in bite sized pieces, so God's Word can be digested one promise at a time. God's word is our spiritual food, we cannot live without it. That is why it is essential for new believers to learn how to read the bible and listen to God through His Word.

Fellowship With Other Believers

Fellowship with other Christians is crucial for the new believer because it allows him to draw strength from others who love God and are growing in their relationship with Him. We should offer to take the new believer to our church or to another bible-based, Christ-centered church.

Encourage To Witness To Others

The new believer may not know everything there is to know about being saved, but they can still witness to others, by simply sharing his or her testimony. It is always good to tell others about what Jesus has done in your life.

Build A Loving Relationship

As spiritual moms and dads, we must be patient and sensitive to the needs of the new believer. It is important that the new believer is in a loving, friendly and encouraging environment. The spiritual parents must care for the new believer by watching over, and nurturing them. All babies, both physical and spiritual, need protection. I can remember how protective I was about my four babies especially when they were learning to walk. Every time that it appeared that they were going to tumble over, I would try to stabilize their fall because I did not want them to get hurt. The new believer is in need of protection from falling. They need to be protected from falling into the enemy's traps. The new believer needs encouragement as he or she grows into a mature Christian. They need to know that someone understands them and takes pride in them. How much love we show, how much concern we demonstrate, and how we relate to the new believer will either keep them or drive them away.

Please allow me to share a story about how a new believer can be driven away. I had a friend of mine who was on fire for the Lord. She had recently joined the soul winning ministry team at her local church. She was praying for God to give her opportunities to share the gospel. The more she prayed the more God answered her prayers. She was witnessing and people were receptive to the gospel and accepted Jesus as their Lord and Savior. For a period of time the church was flourishing with new believers, but eventually the attendance started to drop. Over half of the new believers that my friend had witnessed to were not attending church anymore. She talked to some of the new believers and asked why they had left. The most general response was that they felt alone. After attending the new converts class, they still had questions about their new faith and no one was there to give them the answers.

While I will agree the new believer must take an active role in ensuring that he or she grows into a mature Christian, we as spiritual parents have a responsibility in the new believer's growth process.

My Final Thoughts

J UST THINK FOR A MOMENT, what if no one ever told you about Jesus Christ. You would be lost today. You would be on your way to hell. Glory Be to God somebody took the time to pray for you. Somebody took the time to share the gospel of Jesus Christ with you. I don't know if it was a one-on-one witnessing experience, or if you were in a revival meeting and heard a sermon that convicted your soul, or if someone shared a gospel tract with you. Regardless of the method, somebody shared the message of Jesus Christ with you. Now it's your turn.

It is your turn to tell someone else about the joy that you have experienced since you have accepted Jesus as your Lord and Savior. It's your turn to share your testimony. It's your turn to offer someone hope. It's your turn to lead someone on the path to Jesus. Don't you want others to experience the joy of being saved? Can you envision seeing your loved ones in heaven with you glorying God?

As children of God, we can't idly sit back and watch sinners go to hell. We have been commissioned to fulfill the Great Commission. We must view this endeavor as something that is of upmost importance and keep it on the forefront of our agenda because there are too many people who are living without hope. They live without hope because they don't have Christ in their lives. It's up to us to give hope, and that hope lies in having a loving relationship with Jesus. Somebody is waiting for you to show them the right way, and the only way, is the way that leads to Jesus. Have you been fishing lately?

A Sinner's Plea

O Christian man, woman, boy and girl,
I long to hear your salvation story.
To learn about God's love, His goodness, and His glory.
Please tell me how can I ever grow
If I am constantly pushed aside, tossed to and fro.
Seasoned saints why won't you talk to me,
Why do you leave me alone?
Instead of praying and leading me to the throne.
You say that you care that I am lost and on my way to hell
But based on your actions it's really hard to tell.
Will you embrace me and show me the way,
Or will you put it off for just one more day?
I am searching for answers because I have no peace inside.
Please don't pass me by and push me aside.
Because I look to you as my spiritual guide.
There is a choice that I must make.
Will I go to heaven or will I burn in the lake?
I want to be taught so I can understand.
How to change my ways and live as a righteous man.
If only you lived what you taught and preached,
My soul and so many others could be reached.
I am waiting on you to tell me the
story of how Jesus died on the cross for me.
How on the third day he rose, so I could be free.
I want to be ready when he comes back again.
Living holy and free, forgiven of my sins.
I know it's up to me where I spend eternity.
But I need you to lead and guide me,
so I can make heaven my destiny.
This is a sinner's plea.

By Angela R. Camon